Are you the Next Target of Cyber Criminals? - Practical Tips and Guide in a layman's language.

Cyber Security Demystified for non-techie, organizations, students, teachers, kids, law enforcement, women and for the common man.

SERIES – I

Prakash Prasad

Learn how Not to be phished, exploited, defrauded, 50+ practical tips, Counter ATP, Email Scams, Vishing Calls, Whatsapp Scams, Zero-day Threat, Cloud Security, Social engineering attacks, Ransomware risk, Online Banking Frauds, Dating Scams, PDoS, data security, Tor and lot more.

Table of Contents

By Prakash Prasad

Learn cyber security basic hygiene to advance defense, simple tips to powerful security, Bitcoin scams, protection against sensitive data theft, tips to counter social engineering threats, IoT, tips to protect your hard earned money, stay safe from cyber con artist and much more!

Published in 2017 by Creative Space Publishing

Introduction

Are you the next target of cyber criminals? Probably yes! Cyber Criminals are the best con artist who will trick you to do things which you otherwise won't do. The best of systems security will get compromised due to the weak human security. Tons of malicious content flood the internet. This will compromise your system and your device. If you believe that using Antivirus will keep you safe.. You are probably wrong. A skilled hacker can reversed engineer. You, your family and your organization is the easiest target for Hackers - if we don't make their attempts unsuccessful. We love freebies but not every free thing you get on internet is free. Most of them have proven track record of resulting into costliest affairs. A bad coded pdf file or even image file is dangerous. A too good be true offers will tempt you and you will be their target audience. A fake notice from police or lawyer or even banks or regulatory agencies will trick your mind. Best of best protection fails, attackers defraud large organizations, banks and financial institutions. Tons of fortune is lost every year. The hard-earned money stolen and you are helpless.

Give me 150 minutes and I will show you 55 "traps" that led to a stunting cyber crime and cyber attacks...resulting into big financial loss, mental agony, privacy exposed, information leaks and mess up your digital life. Each trap just requires 6-15 seconds of your attention to de-rail cyber attacks and cyber criminal's efforts. I will walk you through the process of securing yourself, family, friends, organization and of course your money! So that you aren't the next target of cyber criminals

If you don't take care of cyber security, you will end up on an average shelling out US $ 20,000. If you attending any cyber security webinar or online course to learn to be cyber safe.. You will probably pay around $120-$350 on an average. Some of the concepts can be too technical to digest as well. My series of book will educate you on the numerous threats and countermeasures to protect as well as to defend the attempts to pawn you.

If you are in serious about protecting your child, friends, family and company from script kiddies, politically motivated Hackers or ideology support groups or cyber threats in front of you. If you don't want to be the next target and If you are serious about your data and confidential information. This book will help you protect yourself from some of the common threats that exist today in an easy way to so that you can have a recall effect. Go ahead and grab the mesmerizing copy to protect your digital life and your bank accounts before it is too late.

Don't fall in love with PDF attachments.

PDF attacks - Easy to exploit, Hard to Detect:

PDF attacks are another easy way to exploit users. A Malicious pdf attachment is sent to the user and is tricked to open the attachment. Open attachment launches multiple attack vectors in a victim's computer. Around 60% of the targeted attacks are pdf exploits. It is the most commonly used file formats.

Malicious actors continuously create, innovate, and obfuscate new techniques. Are in such a way that they could bypass email spam filters, corporate firewall, Intrusion Prevention Systems, antivirus and security controls like proxy servers. Pdf document consists of the header, body, reference table and trailer. The malformed pdf header acts as an attack vector. This PDF document format pawns the victim. Generally, this PDF document is one page might look blank or very big pdf attachments. As soon as open the pdf document a Malicious JavaScript code runs automatically corrupts the system or part of memory known as heap. The shell code is the bad code that auto connects to the Internet and downloads Malware. This Malware is auto activated.

Now, don't be shocked that if I don't open pdf documents I am safe.. No! A pdf uses a compression technique like your zip utilities. Due to this a section of pdf document can auto decompress the Malicious pdf file using file Explorer shell option. Corporate should analyze the pdf document header as well as Metadata to determine the Malicious code embedded. Even employees must be trained not to open any emails from unknown senders and never download any attachments as far as possible because sometimes the trusted sender emails can also be spoofed by the cyber criminals.

PDF Threats Tracker:

http://www.malwaretracker.com/pdfthreat.php

Reference:

- Portable Document Format (PDF) Security Analysis and Malware Threats, Alexandre Blonce - Eric Filiol 1- Laurent Frayssignes.
  http://www.blackhat.com/presentations/bh-europe-08/Filiol/Presentation/bh-eu-08-filiol.pdf
- Rowan Hanna, Adobe Reader and PDF security threats
  http://www.planetpdf.com/enterprise/article.asp?contentID=8359&
- Scott Merrill,An analysis of a PDF exploit.
  https://techcrunch.com/2010/07/23/an-analysis-of-a-pdf-exploit/

Prevention tips:

Disable JavaScript

Curtail access to system information and network resources by blocking pdf readers.

Block web browsers using pdf

Install PDF Reader on an isolated computer.

Use Sumatra pdf utility

Image can hack your Whatsapp Account- Risk, threat and countermeasures:

You are more likely to click on the image of a beautiful woman or a handsome gentleman or a tempting food picture or a cute looking animal. Image embedded with malicious code or an executable file containing a virus or backdoor. We love to use Whatsapp on desktop/laptop /device's favorite web browser like Chrome, Safari, Microsoft edge or Mozilla.

We should keep this in mind - that a backup of the personal data is always created in the system. This can lead to your sensitive data or confidential information leaked. Although Whatsapp had fixed this vulnerability, but possibly undiscovered threats exist. So, be careful while you click on the image or pictures.

During a natural disaster or during any serious damage or accidents the cyber criminals flood social media with a malicious picture of the incident to compromise your system to get access to confidential or Credentials.

References:

- James Frew,4 Security Threats WhatsApp Users Need To Know About http://www.makeuseof.com/tag/4-security-threats-whatsapp-users-need-know/
- DECCAN CHRONICLE | FRANCIS D'SA, WhatsApp could be a potential security threat http://www.deccanchronicle.com/151031/technology-latest/article/whatsapp-could-be-potential-security-threat
- Nitinbhatia.in, WhatsApp – A Serious Threat to Privacy http://www.nitinbhatia.in/views/whatsapp-serious-threat-privacy/

Hookups on public Wi-Fi could be deadly:

Freebies are not always good. It is a general human tendency to get attracted to free things. If you are hooking up/connected to the public Wi-Fi... Is rest assured that someone is stealing your data and eavesdrop your information. Using free, open source software, cyber criminals can easily steal; thousands of user login credentials to their social networks account, emails, & bank accounts, etc. Few Megabytes of data can ruin your life and make your life miserable.

Free Wi-Fi at Hotel, Airport, Cafe, Railway Station, Library or any Public Place can easily expose your sensitive data, confidential file, documents, or business secrets. Wi-Fi itself is not secured. Even a new script kiddie can run an open source hacking tools and crack a Wi-Fi   Password.

The attacker can launch a man-in-the-middle attack when you are connected with public Wi-Fi. They will act as a server between your system /device and the website you are trying to connect. The data passing by is stolen. Cyber criminals use the dark web to sell this data for a premium price.

Security Threats:

1. Data Stealing or Leakage

2. Fake Wi-Fi Network Set up by a hacker with the same corporate Wi-Fi   name

3. Buffer Overflow Attack using Wi-Fi Network

4. Man-in-the-Middle Attack

Tips:

Never Connect on Public Wi-Fi

Use Network Scanners and Intrusion Detection System to find fake Wi-Fi Connections

References:

- Kasperskylab, How to Avoid Public WiFi Security Risks https://usa.kaspersky.com/resource-center/preemptive-safety/public-wifi-risks
- Thegoan, Unsecured WiFi. http://www.thegoan.net/details.php?id=9325
- Lisa Phifer,Top Ten Wi-Fi Security Threats http://www.esecurityplanet.com/views/article.php/3869221/Top-Ten-WiFi-Security-Threats.htm
- JOE GRAY, Security Issues of WiFi - How it Works https://www.alienvault.com/blogs/security-essentials/security-issues-of-wifi-how-it-works

Don't leave your cookies for others:

Don't mistake this with the cookie we eat. This one is a present in your internet browser. Cyber Criminals find ways to exploit cookies. A cookie enables you to move from one page to another page without the need to authenticate it again and again. It makes your move easy. If you are buying a book online... Imagine if you cart becomes empty even before you check out with the book... Cookies help to keep your data. It is a text file containing all information about your current web browsing. Cookies generated by the online behavior put your privacy is at risk. What do you? What you like? What you want?

Most of the cookies have longer TTL (time to live); put it in simple words.. This is their life span to live. Cyber crooks exploit it if not encrypted.

Tips:

Always clean your cookies using utilities like cleaners or ace utility.

Delete the temporary file by typing temp or %temp% in the start menu option and drop it completely.

Use Hash format for authentication passwords or credentials and not being in plain text.

References:

- Cookies and Online Privacy
  https://www.unc.edu/courses/2006spring/law/357c/001/projects/jhubbard/cookiesrisks.html

- InfoSec Institute, Risk Associated with Cookies
  http://resources.infosecinstitute.com/risk-associated-cookies/
- Emil Sit and Kevin Fu, Web Cookies: Not Just a Privacy Risk
  https://courses.cs.washington.edu/courses/cse484/14au/reading/cookies-risk.pdf

You don't share underwear... Then why do you share your OTP (one time password)?

OTP, PIN, TPIN = UNDERWEAR

(OTP: One Time Password, PIN: Personal Identification Number, TPIN: Telephone Banking PIN)

Every minute, about 6 out of 10 people share their OTP with strangers. You should never in any circumstances share your OTP with anyone even if they are your bankers or any other trusted people.

OTP Shared = Money Stolen

Seriously, most of the data breach or compromise is the result of poor password or credentials shared with others. We all must accept the fact that most of us uses the same password with slight variations to login to social media /network, email accounts, and even your bank or credit card accounts.

The Critical Threat to password is password cracking, password guessing, password hash brute force methods, keylogger (a program to steal your password) and default passwords (which you don't change for the sake of convenience).

Some of the security breaches: Yahoo 1 Billion +, LinkedIn 117 million, Evernote 50 million, Sony Playstation 77 million, Target 20 million, Adobe 36 million, Home Depot 56 million, Court Ventures 200 million and the list goes on… The primary cause of data breaches is weak passwords.

Check your password strength at :

http://www.passwordmeter.com/

or

https://password.kaspersky.com/

If you are curious to know how long does it take to crack your password?

https://howsecureismypassword.net/

Note: Don't Use your real password to check the strength of your password.

References :

- Mark Stockley,Why you can't trust password strength meters https://nakedsecurity.sophos.com/201 5/03/02/why-you-cant-trust-password-strength-meters/

NIST Guide to Password Protection:

- NIST Special Publication 800 128, Guide for Security-Focused Configuration Management of Information Systems http://nvlpubs.nist.gov/nistpubs/Legac y/SP/nistspecialpublication800-128.pdf

- New NIST Guidelines for Organization-Wide Password Management
  https://www.nist.gov/news-events/news/2009/04/new-nist-guidelines-organization-wide-password-management

List of Commonly used passwords:

- http://www.passwordrandom.com/most-popular-passwords
- http://www.telegraph.co.uk/technology/2017/01/16/worlds-common-passwords-revealed-using/

Tips to protect your password:

Never Share your password

Never Set-up a password Hint

Never Write Down your password

Create a Memorable yet powerful password

Never Reuse the same password

Enable 2-Factor-Authentication (That is password + added verification method like One-Time-Password or Biometric authentication)

The organization should protect their password hash files to avoid mass breaches

Enable account lockout after three attempts to enter the password. This will prevent brute-force password attack

Never create a guessable password.

Use crypt vetted by cryptographers to encrypt your password.

Never use common name, pet name, family name, friend's name, or any other information available on the internet that you have shared.

Paraphrase password like "bottolivlikeyhadewentyBiksaDon" + use some numbers.

6

IoT: what is it? How vulnerable is it and how to protect your IoT devices?

IoT is an interconnection of devices or objects which has inbuilt instructions to do certain task. The IoT composed of sensors, electronic materials or devices, software, interconnected networks, transmission as well as storage of (data) results to track, control, check, aid, and auto execute instructions on real-time basis based on real-time scenarios.

The Internet connects IoT. It can use WiFi, NFC, Bluetooth, RFID or any other wireless transmission and connection technology, including some of the mobile connection technology like 5G, 4G, 3G, GPRS, LTE etc. or any cloud based technology to connect to the internet.

Examples: Fitness Bands, Health trackers, Amazon Echo, Smart Cities & Homes, Google Glass, Connected Cars(Tesla Car), Weather Condition IoT, IoT appliances, Apple Watches, Nike Shoes, Natural Fuse, Water (Electricity, Gas) flow meters, Smart Phones, Microwave Oven, Baby Monitors, Bulbs, Automated Medical Devices, Emergency Triggered IoT and the list goes on...

Security Risk in IoT:

- The Data transmission happens mostly via unencrypted communication channels like WiFi.
- Password is poor.
- 2FA authentication is missing.
- Misconfiguration of Security Protocols.
- Version of Firmware is openly available.
- No Regular Updates available or no regular patch is applied.
- Leaks Sensitive Data and Information.
- Easy alteration and execution of code. This can lead to Cross Site Scripting, Denial of Service Attacks, Remote Code Execution, Shell attacks, Multi-vector attacks and Advanced Persistent

Threats.

- IoT Botnets make service unable to legitimate users.

Tips to protect your IoT Device:

Use Strong Password.

Keep your Device Updated.

Use apt User Control privileges and Trigger Systems to raise alarm about suspicious activity.

Use strong Cryptography and have a code review done on a regular basis.

Have apt Due Diligence in place for third-party devices and integration.

Use Blockchain Technology to develop robust security solutions.

Collaborate with an ISP (Internet Service Provider) to block unusually high volume traffic (prevent DDoS attacks).

Use Advanced Firewall and Hybrid DNS System Architect.

References:

- Charles Babcock, HP Warns Of IoT Security Risks
http://www.informationweek.com/cloud/software-as-a-service/hp-warns-of-iot-security-risks/d/d-id/1297617
- OWASP Internet of Things Project
https://www.owasp.org/index.php/OWASP_Internet_of_Things_Project#tab=IoT_Vulnerabilities
- Ericka Chickowski, Internet Of Things Contains Average Of 25 Vulnerabilities Per Device
http://www.darkreading.com/vulnerabilities---threats/internet-of-things-contains-average-of-25-vulnerabilities-per-device/d/d-id/1297623
- Shawn Wasserman, IoT Security: How to Protect Connected Devices and the IoT Ecosystem
http://www.engineering.com/IOT/ArticleID/12554/IoT-Security-How-to-Protect-Connected-Devices-and-the-IoT-Ecosystem.aspx

- James Plouffe,How to protect the IoT in 2017
  http://www.cbronline.com/news/cybers ecurity/protection/protect-iot-2017/
- Marc Laliberte, Understanding IoT botnets
  https://www.helpnetsecurity.com/2016 /10/28/understanding-iot-botnets/

7

What's on cloud? How it can be breached?

Cloud is not the cloud in the sky. It is a technology that enables us to run devices, application and software over the internet. You just need to login or access the cloud apps using an internet browser like chrome, Mozilla Firefox, edge, etc. Cloud is used for data storage, saving photos, running of various application likes games, software, virtual servers, etc. You would be familiar with include of Apple devices, Google drive of Google, Amazon Cloud Service, Microsoft Office Suites like Office 365, Outlook, One Drive, Adobe Creative Cloud, Big Data, NetFlix, Rackspace, Dropbox, Chromebook, Facebook, Evernote, LastPass, Instagram and many more are the live examples of cloud technology.

You can run your software using Software-as-a-Service. You can customize, create and develop your own application using Platform-as-a-Services. You can rent storage space from cloud companies providing Infrastructure-as-a-Service like Bullet Hosting, Rackspace, Google, Amazon web service and so on.

Cloud is also referred as Cloud Computing.

Security Risk:

- Sensitive Data Theft via Wapping attacks and Privacy Issues
- Malware Attacks using Cloud File Sharing Technology like Dyre Malware
- Weak Cryptography, Session Hijacking, Cross-Site-Scripting (XSS) and Man-in-the-Middle attacks due to inherited name of its design
- Brute Force password attacks

Protection Tips:

Do have a backup copy of your data in Hard Drive.

Keep your password safe.

Encrypt your password file by using an open source encryption tool like VeraCrypt, AxCrypt, GNU Privacy Guard and Bitlocker.

Have Multi-factor Authentication for your cloud account.

Build Strong Cryptography Model which is in line with all modern web browsers.

Read the User Agreement (Bit Lengthy and boring) but it can safeguard you if there is a breach.

Use Spideroak [https://spideroak.com/] and [https://www.encryptedcloud.com/encrypted] cloud services.

Carefully draft SLA (Service Level Agreements).

Keep Critical assets separate from other assets.

References:

- Forbes, Adam Tanner : The Wonder (And Woes) Of Encrypted Cloud Storage https://www.forbes.com/sites/adamtanner/2014/07/11/the-wonder-and-woes-of-encrypted-cloud-storage/#2272a9d45e4b
- Data-Tech, M Puckett: How to protect yourself in the cloud https://www.datatechitp.com/2014/09/protect-cloud/
- Risks of cloud computing https://www.business.qld.gov.au/running-business/it/cloud-computing/risks
- Understanding Cloud Computing Vulnerabilities http://cloudcomputing.ieee.org/images/files/publications/articles/CC_Vulnerabilities.pdf

- Jeff Beckham, The Top 5 Security Risks of Cloud Computing http://blogs.cisco.com/smallbusiness/the-top-5-security-risks-of-cloud-computing
- Dan Marinescu, Cloud Computing: Cloud vulnerabilities https://technet.microsoft.com/en-us/library/dn271884.aspx

8

HTTPS security be compromised

HTTPS is a Security Protocol for ensuring secure communication over the internet or web.

Programs like Bullrun (Used by National Security Agency) can decrypt this secured communication.

A man-in-the-middle attack (a method of intercepting data traffic in transmission) can be performed on HTTPS. A cookie is stolen (from the web browser using javascript) by malicious hackers from TLS/SSL Protocol (A cryptographic security mechanism to encrypt the data in transmission). The connection to the network is required by an attacker, WiFi, or Internet, LAN connection or Corporate

Internet Access points or Networks to do this attack.

Browser Cache is not deleted when to close the browser. In Fact it is present till the time you delete it. The attacker uses this to do cache injection attacks (a method of attack which allows hackers to alter the certificate warning and pose as legitimate). Sad part is that most of the corporations, banks, big institutions, financial corporations, universities, and even people still use IE (Internet Explorer) Browser. We tend to click-through the warning (Continue to website - Not Recommended or display blocked content or this connection is un-trusted or add a security exception to continue) with allows attackers to hack HTTPS Connection.

To hack HTTPS use Open Source Tools like hamster, ferret, ettercap & wiresharshark.

Tips:

Don't use Internet Explorer and upgrade or merge the system to work on secured browsers.

Clean your Cache and Cookie regularly.

Conduct vulnerability assessment.

Don't Click through the security warnings.

Harden the Network and Corporate Local area Network and watch it on regularly.

References:

- POODLE vulnerability in SSL 3.0 https://www.kb.cert.org/vuls/id/57719 3
- SSL 3.0 Protocol Vulnerability and POODLE Attack https://www.us-

cert.gov/ncas/alerts/TA14-290A
- Man-in-the-middle attack
  https://blog.kaspersky.com/man-in-the-middle-attack/1613/
  https://www.owasp.org/index.php/Man-in-the-middle_attack

- TLS/SSL Hardening & Compatibility Report http://www.g-sec.lu/sslharden/SSL_comp_report2011.pdf
- Critical OpenSSL Flaw Allows Hackers to Decrypt HTTPS Traffic http://thehackernews.com/2016/01/openssl-https-encryption.html

9

FTP (File Transfer Protocol) Threat, Risk & Vulnerability

What is FTP?

It facilitates the transfer of file within a network of computers. FTP works on Browsers to transfer large files or on Network to get access to files, data or software from FTP Server.

Threat, Risk & Vulnerability:

The Security risk lies in its design itself. FTP originally made to make file transfer easy. Now, you will argue that what if it is encrypted? Even the encrypted FTP and non-encrypted FTP stores the file or the data in a plain text. The hackers can easily access FTP to leak sensitive and confidential data, login credentials, files and information.

Most of the corporations have multiple FTP servers. It also fails to capture apt logs to assist auditing.

Countermeasures:

Use SFTP (Secure File Transfer Protocol). A command line program to run, access and store files.

Authentication mechanism should be in place.

Limit the largest size of the transfer.

References:

- Risks of Passive FTP
  http://windowsitpro.com/networking/risks-passive-ftp
- Global Information Assurance Certification Paper,Stephen Todd Redding| Why FTP may forever be a security hole, and what you can do about it.
  https://www.giac.org/paper/gsec/748/ftp-security-hole-about/101645
- Security risks of opening FTP
  https://unix.stackexchange.com/questions/232636/security-risks-of-o pening-ftp
- Vulnerabilities in FTP Service for Internet Information Services Could Allow Remote Code Execution (975254)
  https://technet.microsoft.com/en-us/library/security/ms09-053.aspx
- FTP Network Vulnerabilities
  https://www.acunetix.com/vulnerabilities/network/ftp/

10

Online Job, Friendship Club Fraud and Dating Scams

Lucky champ... got a job offer ...

Note the key words:

Eased eligibility or selection criteria, interview with chat messages, adjustable timings, work from home, part-time online jobs, spelling and grammatical errors, offer letter sent via personal email like gmail, rediffmail, hotmail, yahoomail etc. great salary - USD 150 per hour (assume you work for 5 hours a day, you make USD 750 a day and about USD 22,500 a month) sounds great!

CAUTION! The Fraudster is setting up ground to cheat you.

A short Story of Online Job Scam:

Huruta LLC (a fake company) advertises a job opening on their recently designed professional looking websites.

The email is sent to random 20,000 email addresses from email id hurutallcHR@gmail.com.

Eligibility: Graduate with knowledge of Facebook messenger.

Payment: USD 25,000 pm. Interview on Hike Messenger.

Offer Letter: Post submission of all documents, bank details, and identity documents.

1,000 responses out of 20,000; Now, they will trick them will offer letters, original looking documents and legal agreements or job contracts. Gradually they will start charging fees for some verification, short grooming tutorial, clearance certificate and so on.

Malicious hackers top the Google search ranking with their malicious advertisements for government jobs or job offer online. The main motive for them is money.

Red Flags:

- Never apply for online jobs on not legitimate company or government websites.
- Check for Spelling errors
- The Easy selection process could be tricky to lure you.
- Job providers (legitimate ones) will never take money from you for any type of processing or checking fees. They get paid by the recruiting companies directly.
- Avoid greed.
- Never trust a scanned copy of offer letters, job contracts and agreement.
- Always pay attention to email id from which the email is sent.

Friendship Club Fraud:

Many of the married, unmarried and busy business class people are their main target.

They promise you to offer few contacts with whom you can chat and get into a physical relationship. They are set up to defraud you.

Regardless of their claim and guarantee for the good contacts. They are bunch of smarty's to steal your money. Stay safe and please don't be a victim.

Dating Scams:

If you just Google dating websites or apps...about 1.12 core results. These are present to cheat you. Their main motive is to sell your private personal information at a high price on dark net. Most of these are fake or fraud websites.

Any dating app you install makes your sensitive data available for cyber criminals. These apps ask you to give multiple permissions so that they could get administrative privileges (highest level of access). These dating apps use your Facebook login credentials or even LinkedIn. Please don't be fooled to trust these apps. A quick pleasure to explore relationship could prove deadly.

Some of the dating profiles will offer you high society call girls for a premium amount to date with them. They will ask you to pay 50 % by paytm, mobikwik or any wallet payment method. They fool you as soon as you pay them. Now, forget the amount you paid. But, my question to you is about why do you need to get indulge in acts which you can't disclose or discuss with anyone. Don't be a victim of cyber fraud.

11

Bot is not so hot! - Threats, protection and defense for you and your family, friends and organization.

Bot (Bot Root or Webroot or Zombies) is a small application or program written by skilled cyber criminal to take charge of your system. Bot is a single computer or device in a network of bots known as Botnets.

Botnet is a network of infected computers or devices to perform malicious cyber attacks like Distributed-Denial-of-Services (DDoS), Click Frauds, Targeted attacks, to send tons of spam emails, to infect systems to obtain important and confidential data, the bot owner called the command center (Bot commander or Botmaster or bot herders or CnC- Command-and-Control-Centre or boat operator) is the nodal power house to instruct inflected systems in the botnet network to perform any operation or task without the user's knowledge (e.g; collecting data, monitoring network traffic, eavesdropping email, monitoring key strokes like a keylogger application or tracking of every single thing you do on your system. This is extremely dangerous as the crime is being committed using bot infected systems. Any IoT devices can easily infected by the botnet.

Infection Methods:

- Visiting a malicious website resembles as legitimate websites
- Downloading pro-software or paid software free of cost from a torrent website
- Inflected spam email (silently install bot)
- Looks for Security Vulnerability in the systems and exploit it to spread across the network.

Motives:

- Earn big quantum of money
- Bring down Business Rival's Business
- Spread spam
- Conduct large-scale attacks
- Disrupt internet and network functioning
- Create Panic and fear
- Distribute viruses, spyware, scareware and crimeware.
- Steal Sensitive Bank Credentials like login, password, credit and debit card numbers.
- Cyber Terrorist to extort ransom or money

Protection Tips and defense for you and your family, friends and organization:

Reduce User right and privileges when online.

Don't trust email attachments from unknown senders.

Never download or install software or games from torrents.

Be careful before you click on unknown or new website link.

Regularly update your system or machine.

Create awareness.

References:

- Configuring User Rights
  https://technet.microsoft.com/en-us/library/dd277404.aspx
- Conficker Worm: Help Protect Windows from Conficker
  https://technet.microsoft.com/en-us/security/dd452420.aspx
- Updated MyDoom Responsible for DDOS Attacks, Says AhnLab
  http://www.pcworld.com/article/168032/updated_mydoom_responsible_for_ddos_attacks.html
- Policy Brief: Botnets by Internet Society
  http://www.internetsociety.org/policybriefs/botnets

- Online Attack Hits US Government Websites
  http://www.pcworld.com/article/16802
  5/online_attack_hits_us_websites.html

12
Antivirus & free Antivirus: The Fake Zone of Security.

About 60,000 new variants of malware are released on the internet daily. You are always under the illusion that 'anti-virus means no-virus.

The anti-virus works to detect virus contamination, but they are not capable to counter the new malware released every day. Due to the advanced nature of malware or viruses, most of the antivirus signatures get released only after 72 hours of infection.

Free antivirus is designed to trick you to install malicious program. Further, Fake Antivirus scanner will highlight problems in your system which have been never present (Commonly known as scareware) to rob money from you.

Antivirus: the fake zone of security. The antivirus industry today can't guarantee your system security as the antivirus code can be reverse engineered by skilled programmer or malicious hacker. Their growing nature of complexity had nailed down many big antivirus companies. Flame Virus is successful in creating a high-profile attack on advanced government systems and organizations. Cyber criminals from Iranian and Russian Federation are designing complex malware whose antivirus signatures is near to impossible to develop and even if it is developed a new variety of malware blossoms. A single defence can fail but multi-defence can help in making hacker's attempt unsuccessful.

Check fake antivirus:

http://www.spywarewarrior.com/rogue_anti-spyware.htm

References:

- Robert Bruce, IS ANTIVIRUS SOFTWARE REALLY DEAD? http://www.whymeridian.com/blog/is-antivirus-software-really-dead
- Stephen Cobb, The massive lie about anti-virus technology https://www.grahamcluley.com/massive-lie-anti-virus-technology/
- Herb Weisbaum,How to avoid a nasty fake antivirus scam http://www.nbcnews.com/id/44523031/ns/business-consumer_news/t/how-avoid-nasty-fake-antivirus-scam/
- Tom Simonite,The Antivirus Era Is Over, MIT Technology Review https://www.technologyreview.com/s/428166/the-antivirus-era-is-over/

13
Endpoint protection - End Zero Day

Every wants to run their business application 'on the go'

Email, Application Software, and Productivity apps are required to be installed on the mobile devices, laptops and smart tabs or tables. These devices are prone to cyber threats. The Security Policies of company will not allow these devices to work in their desired ability. So they are more prone to malware infection. In order to swiftly detect, watch, alert and stop these attacks - endpoint protection is essential.

Every wants to run their business application 'on the go' Endpoint protects the end point, i.e.; it protects the network and various components like PC, laptop, devices, swiping terminals (POS), Access Points, Application, corporate devices, mobile phones, tablets, scanners, and other virtual OS or devices attached to a computer or network or even stand alone devices from zero-day attacks (an attack type which was not known or discovered earlier).

Every wants to run their business application 'on the go' An attacker is successful in sending spoofed packets through the network, but the endpoint protection will uncover it. This makes the attackers attempt unsuccessful. Also, the zero-day-vulnerability cannot be exploited.

Endpoint runs on dynamic machine learning algorithms which is constantly updated and upgraded. This gives an edge over anti-virus and firewall protection. Intelligent enough to highlight espionage, cyber threats (bugs and security vulnerabilities), and easy targets which were unknown.

Endpoint protection offered by:

- Malwarebytes
- Symantec
- Kasypersky
- Sophos
- Microsoft System Center

References:

- Kelly Jackson Higgins, The Rebirth Of Endpoint Security http://www.darkreading.com/endpoint/the-rebirth-of-endpoint-security/d/d-id/1322775
- Chris Poulin, What Retailers Need to Learn from the Target Breach to Protect against Similar Attacks https://securityintelligence.com/target-breach-protect-against-similar-attacks-retailers/
- Endpoint Security Infographic https://www.promisec.com/blog/endpoint-security-infographic/
- Endpoint Protection for Mac Guide

https://www.cmu.edu/computing/softw
are/all/scep/scep-guide.pdf

A disclaimer: Author is not endorsing any of
these products.

14
Know how Firewall catch fire (Security holes)

You go inside your room by unlocking the door lock. The security guard at the entrance gate keeps a watch on who is coming and going. Same way, the firewall keeps tab on who is accessing your computer over the internet. The malicious hackers, viruses and other types of threats can easily enter your system via the internet. The firewall does keep them away, but is not foolproof.

A firewall is a hardware based (the one present inside your WiFi Routers) or software based (the one present on your PC).

Thousands of Security threats are present in a firewall. Here is a proof.

- https://tools.cisco.com/security/center/

viewAlert.x?alertId=39129
- http://www.cisco.com/c/en/us/support/ docs/csa/cisco-sa-20111005-fwsm.html
- https://tools.cisco.com/security/center/ content/CiscoSecurityAdvisory/cisco- sa-20130410-fwsm
- http://www.thewhir.com/web-hosting- news/security-hole-discovered-in- symantec-firewall
- http://www.securityfocus.com/news/40

Port 80 and Port 443 is always open for hackers to gain access to your system. The hackers exploit the un-patched applications.

The vector of attacks has become more complex. Hence, to protect both internet traffic and application software requires multi-layer security solution.

References:

- Firewalls Complete - The APIs Security Holes and Its Firewall Interactions http://www.windowsecurity.com/whitepapers/firewalls_and_VPN/Firewalls_Complete_The_APIs_Security_Holes_and_Its_Firewall_Interactions.html
- NSA Helped British Spies Find Security Holes In Jupiter Firewall https://theintercept.com/2015/12/23/juniper-firewalls-successfully-targeted-by-nsa-and-gchq/
- Linux Magazine, Holes in Firewall-1 http://www.linux-magazine.com/Online/News/Holes-in-Firewall-1
- O. Okumoku-evroro, Internet Security: The Role of Firewall System http://www.academia.edu/334946/INTERNET_SECURITY_THE_ROLE_OF_FIREWALL_SYSTEM
- Marcus J. Ranum, Thinking About Firewalls http://csrc.nist.gov/publications/secpubs/fwalls.pdf
- Book Firewalls Don't Stop Dragons

14
Stinking passwords

Result of Google Search:

Most commonly used passwords...

- 123456
- password
- 12345678
- qwerty
- abc123
- 123456789
- 111111
- 1234567
- iloveyou
- adobe123
- 123123
- admin
- 1234567890
- letmein
- photoshop
- 1234
- monkey
- shadow
- sunshine

- 12345
- password1
- princess
- azerty
- trustno1
- 000000

Time required cracking passwords:

Check it out from the below link:

https://www.grc.com/haystack.htm

Don't use your original password.

Some of the high-profile hacking is successful because you use 'stinking passwords'. Easy to guess password is a nightmare and simplifies the task of cyber criminals.

If you are serious about your privacy, data, and confidential records - Don't use 'stinking password' (easily hackable and guessable password).

Interesting **free course** on How to remember every password on udemy by Bill Aronson, Tom Cassidy, Dr R. Andrew Bean:

https://www.udemy.com/how-to-remember-every-password/

15

Call frauds and Card Cloning - Don't lose your hard earned money

You share your card details with strangers whom you trust to be legitimate. Think for a minute. Think for a movement... Why will bank, or for that matter any agency need to verify your card details (No bank in the word or Card provides companies ask for confidential security credentials like expiry date, card number, pin code, social security number, cvv number or the 3 digit code on the reverse of the card, One time Password or High Security Code)?

The cyber criminals are telemarketers who will call you to get yours:

CVV Number or

Security Code PIN or

OTP Password Expiry Date on the Card

Alert! Don't be a Victim...

- They create a sense of urgency for you to act quickly
- They offer freebies like a foreign trip, bonus reward points, free hotel stays, beautiful goodies etc.
- They give you a coupon code, bumper prize, lottery prize, a gift hampers, a cash prize of US $ two million or an amount you had never dreamt of.

- They will ask you to pay a small maintenance and handling fees for postage, courier, parcel or some legal (custom) clearance charges.

- They will trick you to share your Bank details like Bank account number & Credit or Debit or Travel (Prepaid) Card Number.

- They will arrange a courier to pick up your check (cheque) or even cash from the doorstep.

- They will ask you to keep this information confidential and don't talk about it to anyone you know or even your lawyers, banks, consumer court or protection agencies, police etc.

- They will ask you not to give any reference and don't need to know much about them.

- They will lure you with no pain all gain offer.

- They will keep an expiry date of the offer or a timeline to comply with the requirements.

Preventative Tips:

Don't pay for free stuff.

Don't pay till you actually receive the goods and services promised.

Don't share any bank or card details with

anyone. Even if the person claims to be from RBI,FBI,CBI,CID or any law enforcement agencies, bank or Credit card companies.

Don't rely on documents attached in an email. They are created using computer based document editing tools.

Don't rely on phone calls even if is seems to be from legitimate voice. The voice is spoofed using computer or tools available on the internet.

Don't trust anyone over the invisible channels.

Don't trust anyone on Social Media unless their credentials are endorsed.

Don't trust companies or individuals who force you to act in a time bound manner.

When in doubt, ask people around whom you know. Check with the local police or bank or on knowledge forums like Quora if you don't know anyone.

No insurance companies, banks, credit card department, regulatory bodies like RBI (Reserve Bank of India), SEBI, Demat or Trading Broker, Income Tax or Custom Authorities will ask you to share your details over the call. They will never intimate you pay for dues or certain benefits (policy bonus, rebate, refund, limit extension) over the phone call.

Credit and Debit Card Cloning:

Fraudster attached a small portable device and a camera (to capture your PIN and magnetic stripe encoded data) at the ATM or POs (Point-of-Sale) Terminals known as card skimmers or card corners. These devices duplicate your card details and pass it on the cyber criminals. They immediately prepare the duplicate card. The card ready is used to withdraw cash, shop online, shop at the posh terminals, restaurants, malls, jewelry merchant, or at ticket counters.

The Skimmer is placed between the ATM card slot where you insert your card to draw cash or attach to the back of a POs Machine.

How Criminals Clone your Card (Video):

https://youtu.be/IITY2XukZek

EMV or Chip Based Card are not full proof. They can also be cloned using sophisticated high cost skimmers.

How to detect skimmers or card cloners?

Check the ATM Card Slot for Green Light. If the light is off the skimmer might is present.

Check for loose card slot by touching the slot.

Slightly tap on the keypad attached. Add-on fake keypad will have a bulge touch.

Check if the keypad is capturing your

fingerprint.

Visually inspect the surroundings when you enter an ATM for any unusual holes or light placed.

Prevent your debit and credit card from cloning:

Never use debit or credit card at an isolate places or remote places.

Never use it POs terminals having a small black color device attached at the end of the device.

Place your palm when you key in your PIN.

Inspect the ATM before using it.

Never swipe your card if you feel or smell anything fishy.

Avoid using at places you don't trust.

Never flash at the bar or pubs as the chances of it getting cloned are high.

Never use your card for shopping at un-trusted e-commerce websites.

Be alert and vigilant when you are handing over your card for payments.

Trust your gut feeling.

Develop a secure security protocol using Blockchain to prevent card frauds.

References:

- All About Skimmers, Kerbs on Security
  https://krebsonsecurity.com/all-about-skimmers/
- Taking a Trip to the ATM? Beware of 'Skimmers
  https://www.fbi.gov/news/stories/atm-skimming

16
Trash can crash your bottom line

Trash = Treasure of Information

"Information is power."

Company trade secret is a nuclear missile. The important information is discarded inaptly by many corporations. A wealth of information is exposed to cyber criminals.

In the era of tough competition, your business rivals are looking at ways to erode your profits. Trash discarded without proper shedding can land you in trouble.

Trash may contain your business secrets, plans, proposals, tender, buyer or client list, key stakeholder details, publications, financial reports, undisclosed projects, new business prototype or blueprint, R&D Reports, employee records, meeting outcomes, sensitive data, login credentials, legal contracts, letter heads, source code, vacation details, policies, organization chart, circulars, incomplete letters, stamped documents, signature of key office bearers and so on. Don't be shocked if you meet corporate espionage, frauds, forge contracts, blackmail letters or email, demand for ransom or extortion, competitor launches the product and service before you, suppliers and stakeholders hold back.

Dumpster Diving is the method to rebuild key information from the discarded trash. Corporate had lost more than USD 100 billion due to trade secret being leaked.

Tips:

Create an awareness culture.

Properly discard all trash.

Check the details of the vendor or staff before granting permission.

Ask some irrelevant or unsolicited questions to confuse the trash collector.

Never reveal a password over the phone.

Verify the caller and match with the CCTV footage. Train employees to handle tricky situations.

Conduct a surprise-drill.

17
Nude, Sex-texting & Cyber Sex

A super additive method of texting sexually explicit content (porn, nude, or semi-nude image) using a text message, cell phone & messaging apps. The message can contain nude, photography, video and erotic text commonly known as 'stext'.

Cyber Sex or Sex texting erodes mental state. More and more time is spent. It affects one's sexual behavior, self-esteem, friendship, time, relationship, family ties, job, finance, physical and psychological health.

College goer's teens and even office goers will argue that where is the problem? As soon as anything is shared on a messaging apps or text or mms - it is permanently available on the internet even if you delete it or erase it from the messaging app. The message can be intercepted by the sexual predators or cyber criminals and is passed on to others (create a sense of panic and mental harassment).

Hard Truth: Teens who are sex-testing is more prone to physical sexual activity.

Why do you want to put yourself in an embarrassing situation?.

Why do you want to destroy yourself for a temporary pleasure?

Why do you want to endanger yourself?

Why do you want the sexual predators to harass you?

Why do you share a private photo or video? It could land into a pornographic website just for revenge.

Why do you trust the online stranger?

Why do you want to spend your time, energy and money for a temporary happiness or pleasure?

Why do you need to send your nude cool or

hot among your peer groups?

Why do you want to be the victim of cyber bullying?

Why do you talk about peer-pressure or friends pressure with your teacher, trusted family member or any trusted member?

Safety Tips:

Spend time with your children, talk to them and pay attention to unusual behavior.

Use social network monitoring and parental control tools like safe eyes, unknown kids (https://www.uknowkids.com),My Mobile Watchdog, Net Nanny Social, K9 Web protection, Mama bear app and Pure sight PC.

Don't trust online strangers.

Report issues quickly.

Be calm and talk to someone.

Don't hide details from police they are there to aid you.

Spend time with the near and dear ones.

References:

- Ifran Ahmad,Be Mindful of What You Post on Social Media: What Goes Online Stays Online! [INFOGRAPHIC] http://www.socialmediatoday.com/content/be-mindful-what-you-post-social-media-what-goes-online-stays-online-infographic
- Dena T. Sacco, with Rebecca Argudin, James Maguire, and Kelly Tallon, Cyberlaw Clinic, Harvard Law SchoolSexting: Youth Practices and Legal Implications https://cyber.harvard.edu/sites/cyber.law.harvard.edu/files/Sacco_Argudin_Maguire_Tallon_Sexting_Jun2010.pdf
- Facebook data Policy https://www.facebook.com/policy.php

- Melissa Rayworth, Social Networking Sites for Kids http://www.parenting.com/article/social-networking-sites-for-kids
- A Safer Internet for All - Family Online Safety Institute Resources https://www.fosi.org/good-digital-parenting/
- Jennifer Kelly Geddes, The Secret Life of Kids Online: What You Need to Know
- http://www.parenting.com/article/kids-social-networking
- Meredith Fineman, What We Post Online Is Forever, and We Need a Reminder https://www.inc.com/meredith-fineman/what-we-post-online-is-forever-and-we-need-a-reminder.html

18

Web Site Vulnerability

The Thousands of Websites get hacked every day.

Open Web Application Security Project (OWASP) lists down top website security vulnerabilities (80% Websites are prone to one of these vulnerabilities):

SQL Injection: Let's assume you save contact list in a particular format say Last Name_Mobile Number_Date of Birth. You have saved your contact list in a database system known as SQL Database. Your login details are needed to get access to the contact list. A malicious hacker confuses your system to show the contact list saved by injecting a code.

Cross-Site-Scripting (XSS): Inapt user input validation can lead to XSS. An XSS attack on the website leads to Data theft and the sensitive information stealing. The attacker manipulates the website code (malicious html code or JavaScript) to comprise the website. The remote access is gained by the attacker. A user account is hijacked, dissemination of malware on network is possible and bypass authentication. The attack is can be done both on server-side and user/client side.

Drive-by-Downloads   Malware: compromises the web browser.

Cross-Site-Request-Forgery (CSRF): An attacker creates a forged request and con the victim to give the credentials (buy, sign in, sign out or updating account details) on a malicious website or indistinguishable website from the real website. Browser Cookies, IP Address and crucial information are easily leaked.

Insecure Direct Object References: An authorized user changes the system object (file, directory, url, form, value or database key) to some other object they aren't authorized. The feasibility predicting of numbers or user credentials leads to this attack.

Illustration:

Anu is the authorized user post login URL is - http://www.abc.com/anu/1.php

Attacker manipulates the last digit and gain access to other user credentials. http://www.abc.com/anand/2.php

Missing Functional Level Access Control: An attacker can change the level of administrative privileges (highest level of system access or control) due to poor access control. They can do an action that could be extremely dangerous like deleting files or some crucial part of the database etc.

Security Misconfiguration: Malicious cyber criminals can get access to unused pages, unprotected files, critical un-patched security risks or flaws, default account and much more. Misconfiguration of stack (a group of software or suite) results in this attack.

Using Components with known vulnerabilities: Open Source database provides a description of each known vulnerabilities. This is easily exploited by hackers if not patched.

Unvalidated Redirects and Forwards: An unauthorized redirect and forwards of website can trick a victim to install malware and lead to system compromise.

Security Tips for common website vulnerabilities:

Avoid Special Characters or reject the use of special character to prevent SQL Injection attack.

Use only safe APIs.

Implement Strong Authentication and Control Mechanism. Prevent leaks of Session ID.

Java, HTML Sanitizer Project AntiSamy auto-sanitized libraries can prevent XSS Attacks.

Control and Check Level of access granted to users.

Disable auto-save option for filling up the forms, data and password. Update and audit system regularly.

Assign role specific privileges or access to the system.

Patch the un-patched security risk.

Regularly conduct hardware and software audit.

To protect the sensitive data in a transmission apt encryption mechanism needed. Protect passwords.

Re-authenticate authorized users using CAPTCHA.

Regularly watch and update database to check irregularities.

Prevent redirect or forwards.

References:

- XSS (Cross Site Scripting) Prevention Cheat Sheet
  https://www.owasp.org/index.php/XSS_(Cross_Site_Scripting)_Prevention_Cheat_Sheet
- CWE-285: Improper Authorization
  http://cwe.mitre.org/data/definitions/285.html
- URL Redirector Abuse
  http://projects.webappsec.org/w/page/13246981/URL%20Redirector%20Abuse

19
Plain Text Attacks

If you know the method to encode a plain text, you can discover the method to decode it.

A 'known plaintext attack' is an attack on the plaintext that has been encrypted or may have resulted into plain text file. The flaw in the encryption algorithm can break the encrypted plaintext file.

Example: If you have any of the encrypted files in the zip or archive, you can use this file to get the key to break the entire file.

A 'chosen plaintext attack' is the same type of attack as mentioned above only difference here is that you get to select or choose the plaintext. In other words, the hacker can decide what is to be encrypted and then uses it to break the encryption.

Example: A 'chosen plaintext attack' is XOR encryption. You can choose the plaintext to see the result, so the key used can be easily determined. If you can choose the plaintext and get to see the result, you can use those too easily figure the key being used.

References:

- What's wrong with XOR encryption? http://stackoverflow.com/questions/1135186/whats-wrong-with-xor-encryption
- Vulnerability of SSL to Chosen-Plaintext Attack http://eprint.iacr.org/2004/111.pdf
- Why is a known-plaintext attack considered a complete break? https://crypto.stackexchange.com/questions/37808/why-is-a-known-plaintext-attack-considered-a-complete-break/37811#37811

- JON CANTY, Plain Text Attack on an Encrypted Zip
  https://blog.sandlinediscovery.com/2015/09/02/plain-text-attack-on-an-encrypted-zip/
- Man-in-the-Middle Attack Against SSL 3.0/TLS 1.0
  https://www.schneier.com/blog/archives/2011/09/man-in-the-midd_4.html

20
Pop up Malicious Ads

Pop-up ads are malicious advertisement. A new window containing irrelevant ads pops-up now and then. Of Course they are annoying, distracting and frustrating!

Many ads based companies trick you to get your email address so that they could spam you legally. Why?

Because you had given your consent to spam your inbox by signing up

Malicious pop-up ads can inject or implant Trojan, Virus, Key loggers or even Root kits to steal your confidential data, bank records, documents and important files.

Tips:

Don't close the pop-up ads by clicking on the close button or cancel button because they can run malicious script. Use Ctrl key + W or

ALT Key + Function Key F4 to close the pop-up or right-click on the start bar > open start task manager > select the browser open > Click > End Task.

Most of the pop-up ads probe you to buy fake anti-virus program. They will tick you to install. Don't be a victim.

Turn on the pop-up blocker for your browser or change the pop-up blocker settings (http://www.thewindowsclub.com/allow-block-pop-ups-browsers)

Use Mozilla Firefox or any other secured browser.

Install a pop-up blocker extension from the play store or apple store.

Use Extension like AdBlock Plus, Poper Blocker, STANDS, Adguard, Better Pop, Smart Popup Blocker, Ad blocker, Ghostery, and NoScript.

Don't click on the image, link or website you are unfamiliar.

Use Mobile Antivirus programs like Kaspersky to protect your Mobile phones

References:

- How to stop Internet Pop-ups: http://www.wikihow.com/Stop-Internet-Popups
- Ben Acheson,3 BIG Dangers of Pop-Up Ads and Forms (infographic) https://www.digivate.com/blog/seo/3-big-dangers-of-pop-up-ads-and-forms-infographic/
- Remove Pop-up Ads from Chrome, Firefox and Internet Explorer (Guide)https://malwaretips.com/blogs/remove-adware-popup-ads/

21
WhatsApp Spam

WhatsApp Never sends any spam message, phishing messages or message containing unsolicited third-party offers.

I am sure you might have seen whatsapp message containing (All are Fake Messages designed by cyber criminals to con you):

Offer for WhatsApp Gold

Offer to Join Group of Premium Subscribers

Offer for Free Talk time or Recharge Coupon Ways to disable Double Tick on the message read

Check Account Balance by giving miss call on the numbers provided

WhatsApp Call Invite

Spy service offer to read whatsapp messages of your contacts

Invite your 10 Friends to join a service or offer so that you will be credited with talk time or coupon or discount

Free iPhone or low price iPhone

Fake Voice Call with play button (It's a Trojan)

Rs. 500 off, $500 Vouchers... for doing nothing but just forwarding or sharing a message

Stock recommendation list for quick gains or potential of doubling the money

Update to the latest WhatsApp Add-ons

Forward this message to avoid suspension of your account

Receive message from unknown to call back. They are premium numbers that will inflate your mobile bill.

Take a 3 minute survey to win Burger King Voucher, Starbuck Vouchers or a discount coupon on premium brands. Free Internet without WiFi Connection

Get a free tablet or goodies

WhatsApp will no longer be free

WhatsApp 3G / 4G Scams

WhatsApp Web Phishing attacks

Don't be a victim of falling prey to cyber criminals. Their motive is to trick you to act in a particular way.

Low price loots sale for a limited time. Click on the link (fake link) http://flipkart-big-10-sale.com

Safety Tips:

Never click on any link or play button or add button on the message received.

No one offers free stuff for free.

Never share your personal information and contact information.

Install Apps only from trusted stores like Apple Store or Google Play Store.

Don't forget to read reviews before installing them.

Never share this spam message with your contacts. They may sue you for the loss suffered. Don't spoil other's privacy.

Be alert from the message received from WhatsApp as they never contact you using WhatsApp.

Never share your personal information, contact number, IMEI Number or any other information.

References:

- Suryanarayana Murthy,25 Hilarious Hoax WhatsApp Texts and Forwarded messages http://www.geekysplash.com/2015/05/25-hilarious-whatsapp-hoax-texts-and-forwarded-messages.html

- WhatsApp scams: All you need to know http://www.deccanchronicle.com/technology/in-other-news/191116/whatsapp-scams-all-you-need-to-know.html
- WhatsApp Scams: 3 Things you Need to Kn https://safeandsavvy.f-secure.com/2015/05/08/whatsapp-scams-3-things-you-need-to-know/
- Whatsapp 4G VIP SCAM - Technical Analysis http://www.rafayhackingarticles.net/2016/09/whatsapp-4g-vip-scam-technical-analysis.html
- Look Out for New "WhatsApp Web" Phishing Attack https://sites.google.com/site/appleclubfhs/news/blog/02-08-15-look-out-for-new-whatsapp-web-phishing-attack
- Fabio Assolini, WhatsApp for Web in the sight of cybercriminals https://securelist.com/blog/research/68631/whatsapp-for-web-in-the-sight-of-cybercriminals/

22

Overlooked Social Media Scams

Some of the Scams...

Retweet and XYZ will give $5 Million to you in Donation. (Chain Letter Scams) I lost my wallet and urgent need of funds. Can you please transfer $200 to my account? (**Social Media Cash Frauds** - Cyber Criminals spoofed as legitimate users to tick you)?

Take this survey to unlock your perfect job or partner or to unlock your favorite character. (**Hidden Service Charge Surveys**)

We are always curious to know the unknown. But we end up doing things that prove helpful for cyber criminals. _Example:_ Click on the link http://sly.bit.ly/watch to know who visited your profile. **Fake link to tick you**.

Cyber Criminals flood social media with viral content of a tragedy, accident, event or controversial information leak or video post. The motive behind this is to hijack your system and social media account for carrying out spamming activities. _Examples:_ XYZ Actress Hit by Ferrari, Terror Attacks Virgin, Women, Turtle Laying Golden Eggs, Fish on Tree, famous singer stabbed etc.

Your private party pics are online.

Here is the link:
http://rapidmedia.pk/rea/pics (**Phishing Scams** to gain access)

The Nigerian Scam (popular name is The 419 Scam): Cyber criminals use Instant Messaging or Chat Service on Facebook or Social Media. They create a sense of urgency as if they have lost their baggage, caught by thieves, robbed, or are in serious tragedy, stuck at the airport, legal trouble or may offer to share the fortune of inheritance from an unclaimed beneficiary and the list goes on. They promise to return the money when they return back. Irony is... They never return back and will never return your money.

Cyber Criminals use social media to create lucrative offers for new product, services, offers or some type of contact.

Work from home and earn a decent salary.

SCAM! Your account is blocked, your service is suspended, Your Facebook account is cancelled, Your Account is Charged, Your LinkedIn Account Email Id reconfirmation, free game offers or free version of paid software and so on is a Social Media Scam.

Is this you? Know how mentioned you? (Some random hyper link to tick you to click) post on social media is a scam.

Like or Dislike Power Button is a Scam on Social Media.

Incredible Gains, Huge Upside and Almost No Risk! Guaranteed Returns, Buy Right Now (Pump-and-dump Stock Frauds using Social

Media)

Never overlook this type of Social Media Scams and be safe.

Practical Safety Tips:

Only have Real friends.

Never lend money to anyone if the ask is from social media.

Never Click on Suspicious Link.

Educate your family, friends and create awareness among them.

Never share anything online that can make you vulnerable.

No one offers anything for free.

Legitimate looking documents, legal contract and emails drafted using advanced software.

No one pays you to work from home.

Facebook, LinkedIn, Pinterest or Twitter will never ask you to confirm your identity post first time registration.

Never Click or Participate on Survey or contest shared on social media.

No one will donate fortune to you.

23

Bitcoin Scams - Who Stole My Bitcoin?

Bitcoin is a digital currency. Bitcoin is exchanged using Bitcoin Address and Stored in Bitcoin Wallet.

Since, cyber criminals target Bitcoin because it has gained popularity and high on valuation.

MLM (Multi-Level-Marketing-Scams): A pool of scammers promises high returns on Bitcoin investment. Initially, Scammers will lure you to refer your friends and family to sign up for this program so that you get referral cut or Bitcoin. Later, they will simply loot your Bitcoin and defraud your Bitcoin.

Trusted Attacks and Impersonation by gaining trust and credibility: Bitcoin Logo, Brand and Tag Line are cloned to resemble legitimate. In order to check the Bitcoin usage the user's ticked to enter their private key.

The Fake URL to Steal Bitcoin from Wallet and Install Bot: This URL was in circulation to steal Bitcoin and install botnet. (mybitcoinmania.com/refDirect2412/).
Similar URL or scams is in circulation of social media.

Fee Scam: You are ticked to pay a small registration fees or service tax or charge to convert your Bitcoin into cash. Scammers steal your Bitcoin. *Example*: www.flipyourbitcoin.com/ Scam

Mining Scams for quick rewards: Cloud-mining scam by BitZilla Ltd is the live example of Bitcoin Scam.

Tips:

No one will verify your Bitcoin private key and it is not to be shared.

No Bitcoin Wallet (Legitimate ones) will run a referral program.

No Bitcoin Investment is available.

No one can guarantee you Bitcoin Returns.

Never try to seek help from a dark web for Bitcoin conversion to local currency.

Never Download or Run or Install Bitcoin Miner App or Software from non- trusted sources

24

Malicious Apps

Don't be shocked if your app is evading your privacy, inflating your mobile bill by sending SMS to premium numbers, spamming you with pop-up ads, broadcasting your GPS Location data, reading your secret password, the conversion of your device into a botnet, take control of your email account and spread malware.

Some of the malicious apps are:

Cleaner, Photoshop Tutorials (Free), Cute Wallpapers, TV Mera Live, TV Zurera, NFL Puzzle game, Cricket World cup and Teams, Spy Pro and the list goes on.

Why are they successful?

- Compel the users to rate
- Block your access
- Disguised as legitimate
- Backed by fake reviews
- Deploy key words which users are more likely to search

Safeguards:

Install app from play store.

Enable App verification on by following steps.

Never install app asking too many permissions.

Unknown developer is malicious.

References:

- Protect against harmful apps
  https://support.google.com/accounts/answer/2812853?hl=en
- FairPlay: Fraud and Malware Detection in Google Play
  https://arxiv.org/abs/1703.02002
- Malicious apps, mobile malware reaches 1 million mark [Trend micro infographic]
  http://www.zdnet.com/article/malicious-apps-mobile-malware-reaches-1-million-mark/

25
Secure your secured browser

Web Browser (Mozilla Firefox, Chrome, Microsoft Internet explorer, Apple Safari, etc.) enables you to surf the internet or connect to a web page/website.

Why I need to secure my web browser?

• Higher the functionalities, web browsers will be less secure.

• Discovery of new bugs happens post software installed, configured and complied.

• You tend to click on the link without considering the risk element.

• A legitimate website spoofed to disguise as legitimate.

• The Third party software may or may not release security updates.

• Many of you don't know who to configure a web browser securely.

• Unwillingness to enable/disable functionality as required to secure your web browsers.

An attacker can compromise your system by exploiting vulnerabilities in web browser. A malicious website will passively attack your system.

Let's understand few security vulnerabilities that affect us:

ActiveX: Microsoft Internet Explorer uses ActiveX that allows applications or parts of applications used by the web browser. The part can live in the system or may offer the part as a downloadable object.

Now the problem here is that ActiveX can install any unknown application from an unsecured web page this increase the chances of 'surface attacks' on the client-side-system.

Java:

An object-oriented programming language used to develop active content for a web page. Java-code or Java applets execute within a 'sandbox' where interaction with the rest of the system is limited but the vulnerabilities in Java applets can bypass this limitation or restriction. They always prompt the users before they execute.

JavaScript (ECMAScript):

We love an interactive web page that is the outcome of JavaScript. The vulnerabilities in JavaScript can allow attacker to take control of your system.

Plug-Ins or Add-Ons:

Plug-ins can contain programming bugs such as buffer overflows, or they may contain design flaws such as cross-domain violations, which arises when the same origin policy (NPAPI standard developed by Netscape) is not followed while developing Plug-Ins.

How to Secure Your Web Browser?

Learn how to securely configure the most popular web browsers and how to disable features that can cause vulnerabilities. Important reference resource to secure your web browser:

- Google Chrome: https://support.google.com/chrome#topic=3421433
- Mozilla Firefox: Firefox's private browsing, password features and other security settings, visit https://support.mozilla.org/en-US/products/firefox/privacy-and-security

- Microsoft Internet Explorer (IE): for up-to-date information on security and privacy settings for Internet Explorer, visit http://windows.microsoft.com/en-us/internet-explorer/ie-security-privacy-settings
- Apple Safari: Safari's security settings on Apple devices, visit https://support.apple.com/en-us/HT201265 and for the "Privacy and security" , visit http://help.apple.com/safari/mac/8.0/

References:

- Evaluating Your Web Browser's Security Settings http://www.us-cert.gov/ncas/tips/st05-001
- Browsing Safely: Understanding Active Content and Cookies http://www.us-cert.gov/ncas/tips/st04-012
- Before You Connect a New Computer to the Internet http:///www.us-cert.gov/security-publications/you-connect-new-computer-internet

- Technical Trends in Phishing Attacks http://www.cert.org/archive/pdf/Phishing_trends.pdf
- Home Network Security http:///www.us-cert.gov/security-publications/home-network-security
- Understanding Your Computer: Web Browsers http://www.us-cert.gov/ncas/tips/st04-022-0
- Results of the Security in ActiveX Workshop http://resources.sei.cmu.edu/library/asset-view.cfm?assetid=52712

26
Don't Track Me

Image someone spying on your browsing activity. As your privacy exposed and you feel intimidated. They track your browsing habits to advertise products and services.

If you feel private browsing mode will protect you, then you should recall what happened to users using lulu.com. They place a 'tracking cookies' in your browsers.

Even if you clear your browsing history the attackers can recreate it by a technique known as 'respawning'.

Steps to enable tracking protection:

Internet Explorer > click on the settings icon on the top right hand corner of the web browser > Select Safety > Tracking Protection > Accelerators> Select your permission List > Choose to automatically block (To block all) or Choose content to block or allow (for selective blocking)

Safari > Click on the Menu bar on the top of your screen > Go to preferences > Choose Advance Preferences > Click on the check box 'Show Develop menu in menu bar' (bottom of the box) > Select Develop option > Choose Send Do not Track HTTP Header

Mozilla Firefox > On the Menu bar click on Preferences > Go to Privacy Tab > click on the checkbox 'Tell websites I do not want to be tracked'.

Google Chrome > Install Do Not Track Extension from Extension Gallery

Tracking protection Add-ons/ Extension:

- SafeCache
- Ghostery
- RequestPolicy
- Privacy Choice
- Easy List
- Do Not Track
- Abine

27
2FA - Double Protection for You

What if your years of hard work, planning, database could be destroyed by malicious hackers simply because someone stole your password? Why do you want someone else to get access to your file, photos and confidential project documents? Why do you want the hacker to cause a nightmare?

So, if you want to keep hackers at bay. If you're serious about your privacy and If you care about your data? Go ahead and enable 2-Factor Authentication (2FA).

Steps to Turn-on 2FA for Gmail:

https://www.turnon2fa.com/tutorials/how-to-turn-on-2fa-for-gmail-2/

http://www.google.com/intl/en-US/landing/2step/features.html

Steps to Turn-on 2FA for Yahoo:

https://www.turnon2fa.com/tutorials/how-to-turn-on-2fa-for-yahoo/

Steps to Turn-on 2FA for Outlook:

https://www.turnon2fa.com/tutorials/how-to-turn-on-2fa-for-outlook/

Steps to Turn-on 2FA for Facebook:

https://www.turnon2fa.com/tutorials/how-to-turn-on-2fa-for-facebook/

Steps to Turn-on 2FA for LinkedIn:

https://www.turnon2fa.com/tutorials/how-to-turn-on-2fa-for-linkedin/

Steps to Turn-on 2FA for Twitter:

https://www.turnon2fa.com/tutorials/how-to-turn-on-2fa-for-twitter/

The Complete list of Illustrative Tutorials on 2FA for free can be found here:

https://www.turnon2fa.com/tutorials/

28
Don't allow skimmers to skim away hard earned money from ATM

Guess if tomorrow morning you get up and your Bank account turn out to empty. You are bursting with anger, frustrated and helpless. Why not to pay attention to small clues to protect your ATM Card from white-collar thieves.

ATM Skimmer is a device that records, stores, transmit ATM Card Data / Information. They can use Bluetooth, inbuilt storage, GSM Standards to send Stolen Data using SMS or by physically removing the device installed. They use this information collected to clone or duplicate your card. It is like a plastic keypad or a box like device placed on the ATM Card Slot, Keypad or Card Reading Panel. On an average one looses about US $ 50 k to 70 k.

Ticking alerts:

Inspect if the ATM Card Slot is loose.

If forcefully scratched.

If the slot resembles Convex in Shape (make a C shape using left hand that is Convex) or could be ultra-thin in shape.

If the design of an ATM is too deep-insert your ATM Card

29
Anti-zero-day

Zero-day (0-day, 0day, Zeroday) is an attack which was unknown earlier and now exploited by attackers. The attack is not detected at first place and there is no readily available counter defense mechanism. It remains zero-day attack till the time a security patch is released.

The attacker obtains the code of the system or a program and then performs a type of reverse engineering technique known as Return Oriented Programming. They take a few lines of code at a time and try to write exploit and finally they compile the entire fragment of various exploit and launch a zero-day attack. The exploits developed is auctioned on deep web for the highest bid.

Anti-Zero Day:

Have a disaster recovery and an incident response plan.

Patch and update the system software and hardware regularly.

Use a robust anti-zero day security solutions.

Be mindful of assigning admin and network privileges.

Always use the latest OS Version.

The old way of malware detection is ineffective as they relied on binary signatures or repute outside web URLs and servers. Also, Address Space Layout Randomization (ASLR) and Data Execution Prevention (DEP) is ineffective protection measures.

Collaborate with the security experts and security industry to stay updated with the new type of threats and its countermeasures.

Make your users aware of their action.

Conduct a regular vulnerability Test to discover unpatched flaws.

Don't just deploy application because of time pressure. Get the code thoroughly reverse engineer and check for bugs.

Deploy heuristic Scanners to block unknown attacks.

Use Advanced Analytics Techniques to detect the slightest level of abnormalities.

Robust system to disconnect important system from attacking system could come to your rescue.

Develop a security solution using Blockchain Technology.

If there is unexpected growth in legitimate network traffic is the sign of zero-day attacks.

Consult a Counter-Threat-Unit or any external security Industry for help.

Have software which could shield the application software and browsers. _Example:_ MBAE Premium

References:

- Return-oriented programming
  https://en.wikipedia.org/wiki/Return-oriented_programming
- Zero-day illustrated in this video by Fire Eye: https://youtu.be/-BIANfzF43k
  https://vimeo.com/140163198

30
What's NFC? What's RFID? How hackable is it? What are the protection measures?

Near Field Communication (NFC): Auto-data transfer without internet connection within the range of 4 centimeters. Most of the Tap-and-go or contactless payment services or cards are NFC Technology enabled. A very small amount of data signals transmitted using radio-frequency technology. Examples: Apple Pay, Samsung Pay, Google Wallet, Android Beam, and Credit cards with NFC Symbols.

Security is always discounted for convenience. NFC technology could auto-transfer malware or any other forms of auto-executing threats, if attackers can hack your proximity or accidentally bumps. As there is no security or authentication mechanism in place.

RFID (Radio-Frequency Identification): Is a very tiny device to track the objects attached. The wireless electromagnetic signals transmitted through this device. RFID embedded in passport, credit cards, smart cards, airline passenger tracking, serve as a fingerprint for various products, travel passes, drones, and even in some of the identity documents. The credit card is easily skimmed even if you are in physical possession of your credit card.

RFID can be easily hacked. The drones using RFID Chips can also be hacked.

Side Channel Attacks: A type of attack where the secret key (cryptographic key) from the RFID stolen by analyzing the power fluctuation or by analyzing the memory use patterns.

Power Glitch Attacks: Wherein an attacker can hack the random-private key used to prevent above attack.

Protection Measures:

Use a signal blocker cover to carry your cards.

Design a strong cryptographic key with enhanced security to make it more secured.

Replace physical memory with virtual storage.

References:

- Stacy Cowley, NFC exploit: Be very, very careful what your smartphone gets near
  http://money.cnn.com/2012/07/26/technology/nfc-hack/index.htm

- NFC relay attacks
  http://resources.infosecinstitute.com/near-field-communication-nfc-technology-vulnerabilities-and-principal-attack-schema/
- Sean Michael Kerner,Hacking RFID Tags Is Easier Than You Think: Black Hat
  http://www.eweek.com/security/hacking-rfid-tags-is-easier-than-you-think-black-hat
- Nilay Patel,RFID credit cards easily hacked with $8 reader
  https://www.engadget.com/2008/03/19/rfid-credit-cards-easily-hacked-with-8-reader/

31
One click threats

What you don't know can seriously be a dangerous. One Click threat is a cyber risk wherein a malicious trojan, rootkits, spyware, keylogger or ransomware, screen-grabbers, click-frauds, drive-by-downloads, web injects malware can be auto-installed and executed.

Examples of Malicious One Click Threats (DON'T CLICK ON THE BELOW LINKS THERE ARE MALICIOUS):

www.Winflashmedia.com
www.Killspy.net
www.Asecurityassurance.com
www.IEsecurepages.com

How to Identify/check for One Click Threats?

Copy the URL without clicking > go to wwww.virustotal.com >paste the URL under the URL tab > click on scan

The Final report will show whether it is malicious or not.

Check the URL on below links as well:

http://www.dnsbl.info/

https://www.mywot.com/

http://www.urlvoid.com/

A malicious website will have keyword of legitimate website. For Example: www.facebook.com/login (Legitimate)

www.facebook.login.com/login (malicious)

www.facebook-login.com/login(malicious)

www.faceb0ok.log-in.com/login(malicious)

Database of Suspicious URLs/One Click Threats:

PhishTank.com

URLBlackList.com

http://malc0de.com/bl/

Report malicious software or One Click Threats:

https://safebrowsing.google.com/safebrowsing/report_badware/?hl=en

32
Block ATP attacks: Tips to Deal and Counter ATP

ATP (Advanced Persistent Threats): As the name suggests it is the advance attack which is persistent in nature. Most of these advanced agile attacks carried out by exploiting zero-day, spear-phishing and social engineering.

The motive is financial gains, intelligence gathering, political ideologies, cyber espionage, and cyber sabotage, destruction of information assets, compelling to shut down or windup operation, and strategic threats to corporations, governments, critical infrastructure and national security.

The attack has 5 stages:

- **Reconnaissance:** Information gathering from various sources.
- **Incursion:** Social engineering tactics are used. Trick internal legitimate user to open attachments or click on the link or read a document or malicious PDF to plant a Backdoor and supporting utilities.
- **Discovery:** Deploy 'slow and low' detection tactics and develop attack strategy to conduct multiple parallel attacks at the same time.
- **Capture:** Unpatched system is exploited over a longer period to gather and capture crucial information.
- **Exfiltration:** Information captured is delivered to malicious hacker, professional gangs to develop a full proof exploit to conduct an attack.

Attack Triggers:

- Elevated network activities.
- Many sign-in request at odd hours or late night.
- Identification of Backdoor or Trojan or rootkit to gather data and information.
- Increase number of visitors to corporate premises.
- Presence of Password cracking software.
- Unexpected large files on network.
- Operate below the Intrusion Detection System.
- Increase in outbound traffic over the time.
- HTML Embed Email and Macros Enabled Office Documents.

Tips to Deal and Counter ATP:

Conduct security awareness training.

They can do the right things in a right way.

Conduct mock drills.

Look for Legitimate Looking malicious traffic.

Think out of the Box.

Look for outbound traffic and analyze their patterns.

Keep up-to-date with the new offense and defense tactics to block the new threats.

Has Anti-Zero Day, apt endpoint protection and continuous log monitoring and reporting mechanism in place.

Collaborate with ATP Defense Security Industries.

33

Email scams (credit limit lowered, jobs offers, private venture scams, gold investments, bank account blocked, Lottery fraud, and Notice from police)

You would have used a fishing hook to catch fish. Similar type of invisible and unnoticeable hook is deployed by cyber criminals to defraud you.

Sample Email Scams:

Subject: Undeliverable messages P

GoogleReminder
<coworkman@coopuqam.com>

To xxx@yahoo.com Apr 29 at 10:38 PM

Google

Morgan Foster (Gmail Team) has sent you a message:

4/29/2017

More information click here.

Don't want occasional updates about Google activity? Change what email Gmail Service sends you.

60 Summer Days At Della

To xxx@yahoo.com

Apr 25 at 8:09 PM

We heard it's your special day... Let's celebrate.

offers!!!

We hope you enjoy receiving our emails. If you prefer not to, please click the following link to Unsubscribe

© 2015 Della Adventure

52 % OFF

VIAGRA&CIALIS
<sale_online_20yapu@pharmacy.can>

To

p_988@yahoo.com   p_98918@yahoo.com
p_989@yahoo.com   p_98@yahoo.com
p_98_99@yahoo.com and 14 more...

Apr 18 at 3:00 PM

Or Copy and Paste this Safe redirect Url into your browser:

===> www.morr.trustwebb.su

P No 34369

Elspeth <dhs@americanracing.com>

To xxxx@gmail.com Apr 11 at 3:27 AM

FedEx #34369

We've got a new message for you.

We have sent you a message with the required information.

Equitymaster's Secret to Succeeding with Small Caps...Revealed!

Hidden Treasure

Dear Reader,

Equitymaster has been researching stocks for 20 years, and researching small caps specifically for more than 8 years now.

Over time, we have developed a strategy to identify high-potential small cap companies.

Several of which have gone on to generate double and even triple-digit returns.

Do you want to know the secret behind our successful small cap recommendations? And how YOU too could benefit from them?

Then just read on for full details...

Warm Regards,

Rahul Goel

CEO, Equitymaster

Incoming voicemail, 9:03AM

Whats App Reminder <crossrow1964@meltzermandl.com>

Whatsapp New voice message.

autoplay button

© Whats App

Very Important Notice from Income Tax

The income tax department has found 3 fraud attempts regarding your bank account.

Someone enrolled your credit card for Electronics payment system and tried to pay some taxes.

Due to these attempts, some of your money were lost and remaining founds were blocked.

We are sorry for this inconvenience but this is a standard procedure in order to recover your lost money go through our webage through the link www.it-gd.sk.uk.com

Anti Fraud Department

List of Sample Email Frauds:

http://www.consumerfraudreporting.org/phishing_examples.php

https://uit.stanford.edu/phishing

Most of these email scams will create a sense of urgency to act now, contain spelling mistakes, the form, email id will always differ from the person or organization stated in the email, it will create some type of panic among the receipt like your credit limit lowered, private venture scams, gold investments 300% returns, bank account blocked, Lottery fraud, and Notice from police for visiting xyz website.

Email Scams Identifiers:

- Provoke to act because it involves money or bank account or credit card
- Lucrative Offers.
- Too good to be true lucky draw... Bumper Prize.
- A link to click or download more information.
- A legitimate looking fake documents
- A cheap offer to buy expensive items.
- An enhanced credit limit offer for limited time.
- Card is blocked... Activate it now.
- Suspicious activity found in your bank account. Click here to correct.
- Refund notice declined. Additional documents attached to complete the

formalities.

- Super Saving Deals.
- Best matching services and friendship offer.
- Inheritance remittance offer.
- Huge donation to you from charity.
- Number selected for lucky draw offer cash prize.
- Girl who meets you in childhood.
- Secret company data.
- Confidential files attached.
- New updates. Install now. Limited period offer.
- Bank account Information Technology system upgraded. Test or update your bank details and check for errors.

Ask yourself one thing that why would anyone be so generous, why will bank send you a link to update details, why will enforcement agencies send you notice via email (in reality it is sent only via registered post), why would someone sends you a secret file or message? Be alert and use common sense before opening emails with lucrative or intuitive subject

34
Ransomware: Is the biggest threat to your data.

Tips to protect your critical or sensitive data and information

"Crime is no longer deceptive. It is obvious but you cannot see."

Ransom = Release of something important to you in return for payment of asking money or price or money paid for such release.

Ware = Object or Stuff that is malicious.

Ransomware: Malicious Crime ware or Software that infects and restricts access to data and systems until a ransom is paid. If the ransom is not paid critical data is deleted.

Ransomware Threat Messages:

"Your computer was used to visit websites with illegal content. To unlock your computer, you must pay a $500 fine in Bitcoin."

"You only have 72 hours to submit the payment. If you do not send money within provided time, all your files will be permanently encrypted and no one will be able to recover them."

Rock Solid Facts:

- Just by paying ransom does not offer guaranteed recovery of data. They may ask you to pay more. Many people have never been able to recover the data even after ransom payment.
- Victims who fall prey to them are re-attacked.
- If you pay them you are part of cyber terrorism network. You are funding their criminal activities.

Tips to protect your sensitive and critical data:

Cyber Criminals often trick users to disclose password or click on the virus prone email links or attachments. Educate your peers and people not to do this.

Implement Spam Filters like Sender Policy Framework (SPF), Domain Keys Identified Mail (DKIM), and Domain Message Authentication Reporting and Conformance (DMARC) to scan and protect your organization from email spoofed Ransomware attack.

Apply principle of least privilege and follow it meticulously.

Always configure the Firewall to detect suspicious attachments and malicious IP addresses.

Disable Remote Desktop protocol (RDP) if not required.

Disable macro from ms-office files transmitted via email.

White list application and let them only if it within the framework of security policies. Backup data and crucial information regularly; ensure that they are not continuously connected or directly linked to network computers.

Conduct Pen test and Infosec Audit.

Power-off the device or system affected to prevent further data loss and isolate it from the network.

A website dedicated for Ransomware decryption:

https://id-ransomware.malwarehunterteam.com/

35
P2P threats: All are invited... But think twice before you join.

We all love free offerings. We get excited too to join the network. But be mindful that all invite are not worth. Some of these peer-to-peer (P2P) networks may have invisible threats.

P2P system, both the client and server is a servant. There is no central control server.

The P2P networks have ability propagate or spread or communicate malicious software. In an organization the firewall policy generally does not block P2P Network connections; this opens-up the door for malicious agents and programs to the network.

The information leak and implant of Trojan or Backdoor becomes extremely easy as the outbound connection is established.

Many of us download movies, music. Games and pirated software from torrent search engines. They inherit a malicious program inbuilt into a legitimate resembling software, music or games. The remote access command can be sent across the P2P networks. It also serves as a playground for cyber criminals to inject hack tools, backdoor's, botnets and rootkits to gain access to your system to carry out malicious cyber crime. The cyber criminals stay anonymous in the network to gain access to your confidential projects and files.

SECURITY THREATS IN PEER TO PEER NETWORKS:

https://www.rroij.com/open-access/security-threats-in-peer-to-peer-networks-81-84.pdf?aid=37050

36
Risk Management Policy: How it's an countermeasure for cyber threats and security risks?

Few questions every organization should retrospect because your life blood relies on cyber security risk management policy:

- What is the current level and business impact of cyber risks and threats to our company?
- What is the plan of action to discuss identified risks?
- How is top leadership informed about the current level and business impact of cyber risks to our company?
- Does our Cyber security program apply to industry standards and best practices?
- How many and what types of cyber incidents do we detect in a normal week? What is the threshold for notifying our top leadership?
- How comprehensive is our cyber incident response plan? How often is the plan tested?

Important Cyber Risk Management Framework:

Cyber Security Risk Management is more than just a checklist or tick mark activity. A cyber breach cost organizations heavily. Organizations lose market credentials, reputation, monetary loss, business disruption and loss in stakeholder confidence. Therefore, inbuilt and join cyber risk into current risk management policy and process.

Dependability on compliance is sometimes costly if there is no comprehensive Cyber security industry standards and best practices.

The business impact and associated cyber risk must be highlighted with the leadership team to take corrective action and enhance awareness and accountability for managing cyber risk.

There should be a blueprint to tackle cyber threats and there should be a prompt response, action and recovery to mitigate the cyber risk.

Evaluate Cyber Risk with both short-term and long-term perspectives to develop protective measures to cover and manage cyber risks.The on-going review and evaluation of cyber security risk, cyber security budget, outsourcing, acquisition plans, risk assessment outcomes, incident response and top leadership or executive policies is must for cyber security risk management.

Develop and test Cyber Security Risk Management alternative plans.

Integrate and coordinate cyber security risk management policy with the existing disaster recovery and BCP Policies.

Build a Cyber Security Awareness Culture and share threat intelligence with the external stakeholders. Also, best practices can be framed from the industry leaders in Cyber

Security Risk Management.

Reference Resource:

NIST Cyber Security Framework

https://www.nist.gov/cyberframework

37

Safety tips for Tor users: Checklist for Privacy Revealed

Browser for anonymous communication = TOR.

Tor users are always on the radar of non-privacy advocates. The Tor developers work day and night to make the browser secure to enable anonymous communication. On one hand the cyber criminals misuse Tor to commit cyber crime and to cover their tracks. On the other hand, privacy advocates use it for free communication over internet and overcome censorship for legitimate activities.

A to Z Tor Privacy Checklist:

Stop using the following on Tor Browser.

a. Java

b. Any Audio / Video

c. Adobe Flash

d. Frame & IFrame

e. Microsoft Silverlight

f. Plugins other than pre-configured on Tor

g. @Font-Face

h. WebGL

i. Untrusted Websites

j. No placeholder for Untrusted Websites

k. NoScript to stop XSS

l. Don't open websites through Bookmark

m. Forbid META Redirection inside NOSCRIPT elements

n. Forbid XSLT

o. Forbid <a Ping...>

p. Don't allow scripting in whitelisted subdocuments of non whitelisted

pages

q. Turn Cross site POST Request into data-less GET Request

r. Prevent Internet sites from requesting LAN Resources

s. Don't Enable ABE [Application Boundaries Enforcer].

t. Enable ClearClick protection on untrusted websites.

u. Don't use Tor of Binary / executable file Downloads?

v. Never Search any text displayed on current web page by right clicking on it

w. Block pop-ups

x. irc, ircs, mailto, webcal applications must not be previewed in Tor

y. Never Enable browser history

z. Limit Cache to max of 350 MB Space.

38

Link Attacks

Don't be surprised if you are redirected to a child porn website link or a virus laden web page. Cyber Criminals have innovated ways in which they could tick you to visit a malicious link.

Here are few sample websites indulging into link attacks on users [Don't Click on the below links]:

http://phonenumberserviceproviderlookup.phonelookuptlk.com/

http://newfreeebook.com/

http://www.bestbooklibrary.com/

Websites ending with .info, .ly, .us are proven to be malicious. Not all but most of them.

Link Attacks are of two types:

<u>Plant-attack:</u> The cyber criminals' plants malicious JavaScript pop-up redirects into legitimate webpage. The Cross-site-scripting flaw is exploited.

<u>The page-load attack:</u> The attack is auto-launched with the virus as soon as the page loads. The attack is capable to compromise the network and your system.

Curious to see the Live Cyber Threats and Cyber attacks, visit:

http://map.norsecorp.com/#/

39

Human (Mind) re-engineering: Is the Number 1 threat. Protect yourself and create awareness culture.

Eve tricked Adam to pluck apple and eat even though the access to it was forbidden. Human emotions are the weakest element in the cyber security chain. The best of protection will fail due to human stupidity.

Brains can be re-engineered to think in a particular way. The helpful nature of the human being is very well exploited by cyber criminals. The psychological manipulation is so effective that it can trick employees and even people to reveal sensitive and confidential data.

Social engineering Red flags:

A malicious email link

A notice from law enforcement, followed by a spoofed phone call

A password reset fake message

A security update CD

A pen drive labeled "confidential data" or "CEO Remuneration" containing auto run virus.

A Ransomware or trojanized web links

A threat or sense of urgency to act

A scam online survey

A free gift, trip or voucher

A spoofed call posing as the top management of the company A fake email originating from the CEO or Top Management to Head of the Departments to act in a particular way.

An attachment disguised as .zip or.PDF.exe or .PDF .rar with an inbuilt payload.

A special advisory Your File was deleted or accessed last night. Your service is terminated.

Shipping Receipt attached.

Bank Transfer confirmation receipt attached.

FBI Letter Code: 432

Know who is dating with your boss. Click here.

You will like this. Love letter from Paris Rusa.

Your phone number is being used by xxx.com

A Google doc attack is conducted by tricking a victim to open doc coming from known sources. As soon as the victim opens the doc the attacker trick user to login via Gmail credential.

Safety Tips:

Don't share internal information or information about staff on phone calls even if they pose to be from a legitimate organization. Don't share the company's structure with strangers.

Don't respond or click on a link in an email seeking personal, financial, or banking details.

Pay attention to the website URL as the malicious URL tend to spell errors or slight variation in name structure or the ending domain extension. Example: instead of.Gov or .Can it may have .Org, .Net, .Xyz, .Sea, .Info etc. Always verify the email request from the legitimate company directly.

Always patch your system, have an apt firewall configuration and spam blocking system in place.

Report unusual activity on network or system slow down to the administration team or the Information security group.

Never use the same passwords everywhere.

Conduct drills to check the level of preparedness.

References:

- Nathan House, Social Engineering Example
  https://www.stationx.net/social-engineering-example-2/

- Social Engineering Red Flags
  http://www.albany.edu/its/images/SocialEngineeringRedFlags.pdf
- Clear Social Engineering attacks
  https://www.quora.com/What-are-some-examples-of-clever-social-engineering
- Social Engineering Fundamentals, Part I: Hacker Tactics
  https://www.symantec.com/connect/articles/social-engineering-fundamentals-part-i-hacker-tactics
- Social Engineering, Part Two: Combat Strategies
- Kevin Mitnick, My first RSA Conference
  http://www.securityfocus.com/news/199
- John G. O'Leary, NIST, Psychology of Social Psychology of SocialEngineering: Training to Defend Training to Defend
  http://csrc.nist.gov/organizations/fissea/2006-conference/Tuesday300pm-OLeary.pdf

40
Assess your vulnerability and patch it quickly

Guess if Ransomware like WannaCry attacks your system and you are literary crying just because you forgot or ignored to update the security patch.

Assessing your vulnerability and patching them on time can keep a lot of threats at bay. The cyber criminals exploit the vulnerable systems because the exploit is easily available and security patch or updates are not installed.

Organizations can't afford to lose critical data due to attack by malicious cyber criminals. Individuals can't afford to have sleepless nights. Banks can't afford to lose the critical client records. Stock Exchanges can't afford to lose investors' confidence. Hence, it is extremely important to pay close attention to security vulnerabilities and quickly apply the patch.

41

Super fast exploration targets - office, adobe reader, flash players, Internet Explorer

The Microsoft Office suite offers multiple security patches to keep its user's safe from cyber attacks. But unfortunately multiple cracked versions or pirated version is available for a few dollars. We sometimes forget that these cracked or pirated versions do not provide security updates and may even contain inbuilt malicious application like root kits, key loggers, Ransomware, crime ware or any other harmful spyware.

Adobe Reader is the most used application across the platform and is compatible with multiple operating systems. There are multiple security updates that are still un-patched or unfixed. This enables attackers to exploit your system.

Flash Players enabled remote-code-execution. This makes the flash players super easy exploitation target.

IE (Internet Explorer) is officially dead. The tragedy is most of the financial institutions, banks, large organizations and individuals are still fans of IE. This makes you extremely prone to getting hacked. A cyber criminal just needs to find the vulnerability to attack your system and sensitive data.

References:

- Gregg Keizer, Hackers exploit unpatched Adobe Reader bug http://www.computerworld.com/article/2531323/security0/hackers-exploit-unpatched-adobe-reader-bug.html
- Known issues and bugs in Acrobat 9 and Reader 9 https://helpx.adobe.com/acrobat/kb/kn

own-issues-bugs-acrobat-reader.html
- Known issues | Acrobat XI, Reader XI
  https://helpx.adobe.com/acrobat/kb/kn
  own-issues-acrobat-xi-reader.html
- Track Bugs and Secuirty issues in
  adobe products:
  https://tracker.adobe.com/#/search
- Shaun Nichols,Hackers exploit fresh PC
  hijack bug in Adobe Flash Player, the
  internet's screen door
  http://www.theregister.co.uk/2015/06/
  23/adobe_flash_player/
- ALYSSA NEWCOMB,Microsoft Internet
  Explorer Is Dead as Windows 10 Makes
  Way for Project Spartan
  http://abcnews.go.com/Technology/mic
  rosoft-internet-explorer-dead-windows-
  10-makes-project/story?id=29700926

42

RAT... Smell Awful! : Must know threats and tips to avoid RAT(Remote Access Trojan)

I am sure none of us like the awful smell of the RAT... Similarly, none of us would like someone controlling our system and performing illegal activities or even stealing confidential details and selling on dark web.

The RAT often hides inside the legitimate programs of application like games or software. The entry point for them is through rogue software/utility or malicious email attachment.

The RAT can take charge of your company's server, change the access privileges, expose email, explore hard drive, cloud storage, capture screen, keystrokes, IP, harassment, confidential information, capture your conversation, spy on your password and expose your privacy via webcam, sensitive credentials as per instruct the command server of RAT. RAT has root access over the compromised system.

The prime target to trick you to install RAT is to gain your access to your system to launch a Denial of Service Attacks or to carry out destructive attacks on critical infrastructure and system. Also, large-scale spamming is carried out.

Tips to avoid RAT:

Always download programs or application from the official website.

Never install programs from Web sites like Softonic etc.

Avoid Java and Flash player as far as possible.

Be mindful of what you are downloading.

Don't get ticked by the free torrent version of paid software or games.

Have a malware block list and blacklist suspicious IP addresses.

43
Google Drive Attacks and Threats

Cyber criminals find ways to compromise users. One of the common techniques used by a malicious criminal is to upload a virus file big enough to bypass Google drive automated virus scan. The attachment has malicious program.

Some of them even upload malicious URL webpage with a button to click here or download a file, pdf document or program. The page uploaded redirects the user to Trojan hosting websites. The malcode is executed. This dangerous attack even tricks users to reveal or enter the user credentials and password.

References:

- Kervin Alintanahin, Targeted Attacks: Stealing Information Through Google Drive http://blog.trendmicro.com/trendlabs-security-intelligence/targeted-attacks-stealing-information-through-google-drive/
- Douglas Bonderud, New Google Drive Phishing Attacks Baited, Ready and Hiding in Plain Sight https://securityintelligence.com/news/new-google-drive-phishing-attacks-baited-ready-and-hiding-in-plain-sight/

44

Admin Rights is not the Birth Rights for everyone: Control and Strategies for administrative rights

Imagine, if Prime Minister assigns equal power as he/she have to every bureaucrat or head of the department. Will the country function smoothly? The answer is obviously no... Since, everyone will do what they personally like or feel. Therefore, assigning Administrative Privileges is a challenging task.

Many organizations even don't have proper administrative right access control. The user will admin rights can download and install software, utility or application which can compromise the entire corporate network. The user may not be aware of the risk associated with it.

The apt control strategy and mechanism must be in place to restrict admin rights only to limited users on approval basis. Regular audit must to conduct.

Reference:

- Will Bradley, Why Should Users Not Have Admin Rights?
  https://willbradley.name/2012/02/06/why-shouldnt-users-have-admin-rights/

45
Why should you keep your employees happy?

A disgruntled employee poses the same threat as a nuclear attack. Human beings deserve respect and must be given fair treatment. A mistreated employee will always find ways to take revenge because human psychology is programmed in this way. Happiness triggers positivity and activates motivating stimulus to do better.

Insider possesses a higher risk of corporate espionage, information leak, and hacktivism and cyber crime. It is extremely important that the employees are clearly communicated what the organization expects. The information flow must be precise and interpretable to the lowest level of staff in the organization.

Classified and confidential information must be protected via military grade encryption and should be not accessible to all employees.

History is witness that a disgruntled employee is behind some of the high-profile cyber attacks.

46

Browser Bot: What is it? How it hijacks your data, privacy and launch hacking attacks.

Malicious Cyber criminals find means to issue a fake advertisement. The fake internet ads are created using JavaScript. The Browser runs and execute this no cost malicious script to display ads on thousands of compromised web browser known as 'Browser Botnet Network'. They leave no trace on exit or close the browser. Only way to find the browser, but is through careful examination of browser extensions.

The Browser Botnet Network is created using fake browser extensions or plug-in. The Browser Bot is capable to launch a DDoS attack, Clickjack, hijack a system, do CSFR/XSS attacks, inject tons of malicious ads, viruses, worms, Trojans and are even capable of bypassing proxies.

Reference:

- The Ghost In The Browser - Analysis of Web-based Malware https://www.usenix.org/legacy/event/hotbots07/tech/full_papers/provos/provos.pdf

47

Hacker can compromise your system with QR Code

QR Code is 2-D (two-dimensional) system readable code. The QR code Scanners can open an online URL. The QR Code is encoded with the information or details of a product, service or a contract. It can also execute a binary code and do a specific automated task.

The Legitimate QR Code can be manipulated to launch modern-day phishing attacks. The machine readable Code can execute an automated phishing scams and re-redirect traffic to a malicious web server. A possible automated SQL Injection also exist. Cyber Criminals can easily compromise your smart phones, tablets, device, laptop, steal your Bitcoin, banking login credential, vital data and system by generating a fake QR Code. They deploy social engineering techniques to make this attack successfully.

References:

- Security attacks via malicious QR Codes http://resources.infosecinstitute.com/security-attacks-via-malicious-qr-codes/
- Swati Khandelwal, QRLJacking — Hacking Technique to Hijack QR Code Based Quick Login System http://thehackernews.com/2016/07/qrljacking-hacking-qr-code.html

48

What is Metadata? How hackers steal data? How privacy is at stake?

Data about Data = Metadata.

An information about a web page (meta-tag), pdf file (containing details about who created it, what is the size, number of pages, identification information), mp3 file (details about the release of the file), all data has some other data known as metadata.

The Metadata contains identification information, i.e.:

Geo Location

System of Device used to create data

Time and Date

MAC address or device Identification Number Serial

Information about the ISP or Internet provider

Size and length of data or information or file

Originator, Creator, Transmitter and Recipient Details

Government Agencies and Private Companies regularly track your activity and spy on your internet activities using metadata. Law enforcement agencies profile every individual and even kill criminals based on the metadata.

Metadata tracking invades your privacy and makes you vulnerable to cyber attacks.

References:

- International principles on the application of human rights to communications surveillance https://necessaryandproportionate.org/principles

- GAP Statement on Edward Snowden and NSA Domestic Surveillance https://www.whistleblower.org/press/gap-statement-edward-snowden-and-nsa-domestic-surveillance
- NSA Files: Decoded-What the revelations mean for you. https://www.theguardian.com/world/interactive/2013/nov/01/snowden-nsa-files-surveillance-revelations-decoded

Dating Apps and Security Risk

Not all dating apps are proficient enough to protect the privacy. The multiple permission requests gave them root access to your device. The secret details of your private relationship are not aptly secured. Some of the even sell the data collected for marketing and spamming companies.

A hacker can unmask your private life. So, why to place yourself in an embarrassing situation? The security aspect is not kept in mind while designing this app. Some of the apps are even creepy to pish your personal details. The average price for your personal data ranges between US $ 30 to US $ 500 on dark web marketplace.

If you're still okay to accept this risk and go ahead - you are free to do so. Just remember how personal information was exposed to the public in an Alisha Madison Hack, Badoo App user Account compromised and many more.

Don't get pawned by Vishing Calls and Smishing Frauds

Vishing Calls = Phishing via Phone Calls, IVR, Automated Calls, Spoofed phone Calls.

Red Flags:

- If you ever receive a call asking for your card, bank, reward card number, expiry date, CVV, PIN, Password, OTP.
- If you receive an automated call asking you to unblock your blocked card
- If you receive a call asking for your sensitive personal details
- If the caller claims to update your system or phone via remote access
- If caller asks you to pay a small fee to claim the fictitious gift or prize money
- If caller approves your credit card over the phone or claims to sanction loan or enhance your credit card limit
- If your account is blocked and unblock it via confirming your bank, card as

well as debit card details.

- If you receive a call from the customer support team to share your details
- If you receive calls to enhance or redeem your Insurance policy bonus
- If you are diverted or asked to call on a particular customer support number and prompted to enter multiple critical information
- Cyber criminals use the internet to set up phony automated calling lines or numbers
- The calls can be spoofed as the legitimate caller to pwn you.

Just try to be smart about it. Listen to the conversation carefully. If you are suspicious, disconnect the call. Check with the Bank or Service Provider directly.

Smishing Frauds = Fraud via phishing sms to defraud you

Real Smishing Fraud Examples:

"We want to confirm the payment of xyz amount to your bank account. If you have not given this instruction. Please call immediately to fraud control unit on +1234567890. Quote Reference No. RT XYZ 21123. Don't reply via sms"

"Your Bank Account is blocked. Call us on … "

"Your Credit Card Limit is enhanced. Confirm your existing card details on IVR Response system."

"You won a car, or apple laptop, or a property. To claim the prize call us now..."

"We found virus on your phone. To remote it permanently call us now."

"It is limited period offer. Claim your code."

"If asked to buy some voucher to clear loan or debt in easy way."

"Dear Customer, you have won 20,000 rewards points. To claim sms your details to 55343."

Don't hand over your details to strangers or even if the message or calls seems to be legitimate. Most of these calls and SMS are spoofed to resemble legitimate. When in doubt, check with the concerned organization directly (not on the number provided in the SMS or phone call). Never click on any link received via SMS (It is designed to con you).

51

DDS (Default Deadly Settings)

The default settings can prove deadly as the default configuration is available on Google search. Most of us never change the default password, default admin account settings, default operating system settings and other pre-set settings as well as credentials.

Global Directory of Default Settings, Login, version and Password List:

http://www.phenoelit.org/dpl/dpl.html

The cyber criminals can hack your PC easily without much effort. The default configuration exploitable flaw is already present on the internet.

Tips:

Always change the default configuration or settings.

Always change the default login credential and password.

Google default settings and understand the impact of each settings.

GPS and Privacy at Stake

Geolocation uncovers your location and uncovers your privacy. The Smart Phone with GPS capabilities had made our life easier, but at the same time it puts our privacy at stake.

Our real-time location is shared with other users around us. Some of the apps list your frequent location and visit to certain places. This puts our privacy at stake.

Cyber Criminals can craft attacks based on the GPS location.

Creepy apps on Google Play Store and tips to protect yourself

Will you like if someone is staring at you? Obviously, No! Fake apps appear to be legitimate on Google play store. The cyber criminal develops fake apps and launch on plaster. The innocent looking apps will gain full control of your device including network connections, location, sensitive credentials and of course carry out spying activities.

Millions of people due to ignorance download and install fake apps. Some of the apps look like that of apps launched by government, shopping apps, fake anti-virus, device protection or lock ups. The fake apps inflate your mobile data and call bill. They can even read your SMS and contact list. Spread spam and display annoying pop-up as well as dangerous adware.

Some of them can even clone your sum card details and send the details to attacker to carry cyber crime.

Fake apps are also found on windows phone or any other platform.

There are fake reviews is bought for few pennies. So don't get fooled by the reviews on playstore.

Tips:

Any apps promises to offer a huge discount or unbelievable offers is a fake app

Fake apps will not be in the list of editor's choice list.

Fake apps will have near to zero fake reviews.

Pay Close attention to spelling mistakes.

Check when, how, who published the app. The real ones will likely come up with an update while the fake apps might have been recently launched.

Cross check the reviews from multiple sources.

References:

- Over 40 fake BHIM apps available on Google Play Store; here's how to spot the genuine one
  http://www.bgr.in/news/over-40-fake-bhim-apps-available-on-google-play-store-heres-how-to-spot-the-genuine-one/
- More fake antivirus programs, browsers found in Google Play and Windows Phone Store
  http://www.pcworld.com/article/2156300/more-fake-antivirus-programs-found-in-google-play-windows-phone-store.html
- EZRA SIEGE, Fake Reviews in Google Play and Apple App Store
  https://www.apptentive.com/blog/2014/05/27/fake-reviews-google-play-apple-app-store/

54

PDoS (Permanent Denial of Service)

PDoS are a fast mode Denial of Service attacks causing permanent failure of associated hardware and hardware components. The IoT devices are hacked by cyber criminals to conduct Permanent Denial of Service Attack.

The attack is so bad that it permanently damages the configuration, firmware and hardware. The components damaged by PDoS can't be repaired or restored.

PDoS attack is capable of disabling the TCP timestamps, disable default gateways, exploit hard-coded passwords, brute force Telnet and exposes SSH. Both Linux based devices and devices operating on BusyBox is targeted.

Tips:

Disable Telnet access to the device to prevent PDoS.

Update your firmware.

Change factory default settings.

Network Behavior Analytics in place to detect suspicious activities.

Have a strong IPS(Intrusion Prevention System) and IDS(Intrusion Detection System).

Reference:

- "BrickerBot" Results In PDoS Attack
  https://security.radware.com/ddos-threats-attacks/brickerbot-pdos-permanent-denial-of-service/

55

Cyber Bullying

A nasty, annoying, vulgar, hurtful, demeaning or frustrating, and even threatening email or SMS or chat on social networks, IM and Whatsapp had made the live miserable of young teenager or young children. The cyber criminals or pedophile can't face you in life that why they hide behind the walls of internet to harass and bully young children and teen-ager.

The mental agony inflates when they are continuously humiliated in front of peers, friends and bystanders. Many of them had even committed suicide because of the extreme mental pressure and humiliation.

If you find an unusual peer pressure or threat of online social network or someone is humiliating or harassing you; please feel free to tell your parents or teachers or woman police officer or cyber cell (cyber police or cyber cop) or a nearby self-help group or NGOs. The cyber criminals will be punished for their wrong doing. Do not be afraid of them. Be brave and be bold. Talk to your trusted ones and explain them the problem they will help you.